I Do Like To Be Beside The Seaside

A play in two acts

by

Anne Le Marquand Hartigan

CHISWICK BOOKS

LONDON

www.chiswickbooks.com

First published in 2016 by Chiswick Books
2 Prebend Gardens, Chiswick, London W4 1TW
email: info@chiswickbooks.com, www.chiswickbooks.com

I Do Like to Be Beside the Seaside copyright © Anne Le Marquand Hartigan 1981.

Anne Le Marquand Hartigan is hereby identified as author of this play in accordance with section 77 of the Copyright, Designs and Patents Act 1988. The author has asserted her moral rights.

All rights whatsoever in this play are strictly reserved and application for performance etc. should be made before commencement of rehearsal to email: rights@annehartigan.com. No performance may be given unless a licence has been obtained, and no alterations may be made in the title or the text of the play without the author's prior written consent.

This book is sold subject to the condition that it shall not by way of trade or otherwise be circulated without the publisher's consent in any form of binding or cover or circulated electronically other than that in which it is published and without a similar condition including this condition being imposed on any subsequent purchaser.

British Library Cataloguing in Publication Data. A catalogue record for this book is available from the British Library.

This is a work of fiction. Names, characters, places and incidents either are products of the author's imagination or are used fictitiously. Any resemblance to actual events or locales or persons, living or dead, is entirely coincidental.

ISBN: 978-0-9928692-3-6

Cover image from a painting by Anne Le Marquand Hartigan.

Also by the author

Plays

Beds, *Chiswick Books, 2016*
Jersey Lilies, *Chiswick Books, 2016*
La Corbière, *Chiswick Books, 2016*
Three Short Plays, *Chiswick Books, 2016*
The Secret Game, *Chiswick Books, 2014*

Poetry

Unsweet Dreams, *Salmon Poetry, 2011*
To Keep The Light Burning, *Salmon Poetry, 2008*
Nourishment, *Salmon Poetry, 2005*
Immortal Sins, *Salmon Poetry, 1993*
Now is a Moveable Feast, *Salmon Poetry, 1991*
Return Single, *Beaver Row Press, 1986*
Long Tongue, *Beaver Row Press, 1982*

Prose

Clearing the Space, *Salmon Poetry, 1996*

For Aunt Dan and my relations from the banks of the Boyne.

Characters

The residents:	MISS EVANS	
	MR MULCAHY	
	MRS MORGAN	
	EVA	*Mrs Eva Murphy*
	FRANCIS	*Mr Francis Butler*
The staff:	MRS PRICE	*Matron*
	TESSIE	*Housemaid*
	MAURA	*Housemaid*
The others:	MARGIE	*Eva's daughter*
	PAUL	*Margie's husband*
	PATSY	*Maura's boyfriend*

Time and place

1970s Ireland. The action takes place in the interior of The Retreat, an old people's home on the seafront of an east coast town, and on a nearby clifftop.

Set

The set should have the feeling of void. The occupants seem to float in their own world. This world is timeless. The few objects on the set are starkly real in an unreal world. A modern metal tea-trolley, the large TV set, a crucifix, the fire, these few things are the only reality for most of the old people in the room. The cast are dressed in shades of grey with some white on EVA's clothes. She might have a little subdued colour as well. The two maids, TESSIE and MAURA, have white aprons. One or two of the chairs are occupied by dummies of elderly people. Downstage is the window towards the sea in the sitting room of The Retreat. Apron stage.

Act One

Scene One

Sound of rain lashing on window panes and sound of the sea breaking on the sea-shore outside. Light up slowly on MISS EVANS. She stands downstage right. She is wiping as if clearing a small hole in the condensation on the window so as to peer out. She supports herself with her other hand on her walker. Her handbag is looped on the rail of her walker. The lights now rise on the whole stage to show MR MULCAHY in his chair, downstage left, and EVA who sits at the chess table reading her book. She is in a wheelchair.

MISS EVANS

Cold.

She peers out through the little space she has cleared in the window.

It's so cold.

Silence. She begins to turn very slowly with her walker. She stops to consider.

Maybe today I could get to the fire before her?

She completes her turn.

I would like to sit by the fire.

Pause. She shuffles. She can only move very, very slowly.

A real fire is so nice.

Shuffle.

MR MULCAHY is hunched in a chair, wrapped in a rug. He stares out the window towards the sea, pays no attention to anything going on around him. You might wonder if he is conscious of where he is. He lives in his thoughts. MAURA and TESSIE are arranging cups and saucers on the trolley with a clatter.

MR MULCAHY

It's cold.

Clatter of cups.

It's cold today.

TESSIE and MAURA pour tea and take it to the old people who wait in various parts of the room. TESSIE takes a cup of tea to MR MULCAHY.

TESSIE

How are you today, Mr Mulcahy?

She expects no answer. He accepts the tea without looking at her. He does not look at her or answer.

He holds the cup on his knees but does not drink from it. TESSIE returns to the trolley. Spot on TESSIE and MAURA at the trolley. Bored.

Jesus.

MAURA is regarding her nails. She sighs.

Jesus, it's always the same.

MAURA is regarding her stockings.

Always the same bloody thing.

MAURA is regarding her shoes.

I'm going, I'm getting out of this bloody dump.

MAURA is back to her nails again.

MAURA

Do you like the colour of my nails?

Holding her hands at arm's length. TESSIE doesn't bother to look.

It's not so bad...

TESSIE

Interrupting.

I'm fed up. I'm handing in my notice.

MAURA

You keep saying that.

She wiggles an ankle.

But you never do it.

TESSIE

I'm pissed off with old people...

MAURA

Interrupting.

Do you think my ankles have swelled?

TESSIE

Paying no attention.

This time is different. Mick's after offering me a job.

MAURA

Jeering slightly.

What! Mick at the shop? I wouldn't work for that old feller.

Stops looking at her ankles.

They say that they swell, at this time of the month, before 'your friend' you know? Mick's an old bastard.

TESSIE

It'd be more gas than this dump.

MAURA

He'd never stamp your cards.

TESSIE

>He would mine. He fancies me.

MAURA

>Janey mac, he fancies everyone. He's the one they say forgot he had a fag in his mouth when he tried to kiss Mary Byrne after a dance. And he's ancient. About forty.

TESSIE

>Oh you can talk. I think you fancy some of the old crabs in here.

MAURA

>No, I don't. I just like them. They're like old babies. Mr Butler's gorgeous.

TESSIE

>I think he's mad. Wait till I tell you what he was doing the other morning. There, in the garden, going like the clatters in that wheelchair of his, round and round the goldfish pond. And that one, Mrs Murphy, egging him on and counting the rounds he'd done. They're soft in the head if you ask me.

MAURA

>They have great craic together.

TESSIE

> And he was as pleased as punch that he'd done eleven!
>
> *Pause.*
>
> Told me I should get myself out of here. Why did I want to be stuck with the likes of them? 'Go off and see the world,' he says. 'What's a nice girl like you doing in a place like this?' he says. He can say that again. And he says he'll give me something. Some old picture he has up in his room. Says it's worth a few bob.

MAURA

> Would you believe that?
>
> *Pause.*
>
> Anyway, I'm going out with Patsy.

TESSIE

> *A bit jealous and surprised.*
>
> Him!
>
> *Pause.*
>
> Janey, you'd better watch it. He was going out with Rose Callaghan and she's just gone to England in a hurry.

MAURA

    So what?

TESSIE

    You know what. Everybody's saying in the village...

MAURA

    They're always saying something in the village.

    Silence. MAURA is pushing the cuticle back on her nails.

    You know what?

    Giggles.

    Matron told me to wear a bra.

TESSIE

    Oh, she's just jealous. If she let hers out they'd drop to her knees.

MAURA

    Ah stop it, Tess. She's not so bad.

    MAURA is now looking at the nails on her other hand.

TESSIE

    Janey it's always the same bloody thing.

Silence.

MAURA

> *Holding out her hand to admire the nail polish.*
>
> Do you like the colour?
>
> *TESSIE pays no attention.*
>
> Ah it's not so bad.

TESSIE

> Jesus.
>
> *Lights up to reveal MR MULCAHY and EVA who sit at the chess table.*

MR MULCAHY

> It's cold.
>
> *Whining. He fidgets with his rug, now trying to tuck it in, now un-tucking it. Still gazes out the window.*
>
> *Enter MATRON. She crosses downstage and makes some adjustment to the curtain or window.*

MATRON

> How are we, Miss Evans?
>
> *She does not wait for an answer.*
>
> Mr Mulcahy, I see you're fine... fine...
>
> *MR MULCAHY takes no notice. She goes upstage*

and smiles and nods at the occupants.

Straightens a cushion that does not need attention.

Ah, Mrs...

She is looking at EVA.

Dreadful day... Just dreadful.

Turns to the trolley and inspects it with an eagle eye.

Now girls, have you everything? Get more scones, Tessie. You need more scones. Right.

MATRON exits. TESSIE and MAURA exchange glances. TESSIE exits.

TESSIE

Muttering.

The old bat.

MAURA continues to serve tea.

MR MULCAHY

Grumbling, whining, complaining.

It's cold today.

He shuffles his knees together. Takes a sip of tea.

Rotten tea. Ghastly.

> *Pause. TESSIE returns with scones.*
>
> She never could make a good cup of tea.
>
> *Pause.*
>
> An idiot woman, my dear sister. She'd insist on making tea by the drawing room fire. Insist. With all her little gadgets. Patty in the kitchen could make a great cup, a grand cup. That wasn't good enough. Oh no, no. My sister said servants just don't understand about tea. She had to do it herself. With her la-di-da tea kettle and caddy.
>
> *Pause.*
>
> She'd ring the bell
>
> *Mimics.*
>
> 'You can bring up the tea things now, Patty,' she'd say. Such a stupid fuss to make a bad cup of tea. God almighty. Made a bloody ceremony out of it.
>
> *Pause.*
>
> All women are whores.

MISS EVANS

> Maybe I will sit by the TV.
>
> *Pause.*

Perhaps it would be better to sit by the TV.

Pause.

It's not so far to the chair by the TV.

She shuffles towards the TV.

I would like to get to the fire before her. A fire is so nice. Nice to sit by the fire.

Pause.

No, it's much nearer to the chair by the TV.

Silence.

MR MULCAHY

He has put down his cup and slowly rubs his knees...

Sings to the tune of 'Any Old Iron.'

>Any old bones,
>
>Any old bones,

That's what I've got, old bones. Old rag and bone man... Aching and aching. My own background music. A golden aching oldie.

Sings to the tune of 'Where did you get that hat?'

>Where did you get that ache?
>
>Where did you get that pain?

Silence.

MISS EVANS

>But I'd prefer the fire. I'd much prefer to sit by the fire. That would be nice.
>
>*Pause.*
>
>Everyone feels better by the fire.

MR MULCAHY

>*His fingers twisting and twining the mohair rug.*
>She was there. She was there in the background. Whispering. Her with her china tea.
>
>*Mimics.*
>
>'The servants just don't appreciate the subtleties, so I have to do it all myself.'
>
>*He sighs.*
>
>Her dear little sensitive sighs, her talking and talking. She never stopped talking, changing everything with her fiddly white fingers. Changing everything, interfering so I couldn't manage. Couldn't do anything, couldn't go anywhere, couldn't go...
>
>*Comes back to reality.*
>
>But I'm not going anywhere. I'm sitting in this chair, a rug of mohair around my knees.

He peers over at his knees.

Those knees.

He almost laughs.

Don't seem mine, so cold and a long way away.

Pause.

Did she give me this rug? Just like her to choose mohair. Long fussy stuff. Interfering.

Mimicking.

'Dickey, Dickey, the horses were on the lawn last night. They make those dreadful holes with their hooves. I've asked you again and again to see to the fences. It's not much to ask. It's only a small thing to ask. You could see to that at least… surely you could manage that… a little thing like that?'

Silence.

MISS EVANS

Matron thinks I'm managing very well with this walker. 'You're managing very well, Miss Evans,' she says. 'Very well.'

MR MULCAHY

I could never get away. She'd always find me out.

Pause.

Even as a child she knew. Knew all my special places. Interfering.

Pause.

Except once. Once in the trees. She never found me there. I beat her that time. Up in the chestnut tree.

Silence.

MISS EVANS

> I used to find twigs for the fire under the trees. Lying on the grass under the trees. The rooks dropped them building their nests. I felt sorry for them when they'd gone to so much trouble getting them up there. But it was handy for me.
>
> *She shuffles on.*
>
> Very handy.
>
> *Pause.*
>
> Sometimes I would collect them along the back hedge. Not in the wood. Mother said not to go in the wood. 'You never know what would be in a wood,' Mother said.
>
> *Silence.*

MR MULCAHY

> *Staring at the crucifix that hangs on the wall.*

You there! You didn't dare to try old age did you? Old age.

Scathing.

What do you know about it, Jesus Christ?
Nothing. You popped it young. In your prime, a bloody hero.

Pause.

Died for us. Died for us? I didn't want you to die for me. You just go along and die for someone else. Not for me, thank you very much. How dare you die for me!

Pause.

I don't want your bloody death hanging round my neck.

Silence.

I had to look at your bleeding picture. She made me. 'Sweet Jesus died for you,' she'd say. 'For your sins. Your wicked sins made sweet Jesus die for you. Jesus died on the cross for your sins.'

Pause.

Blackmail. Your death hasn't done me any good. Hasn't done anyone any good. Opening the gates of heaven with your blood. Funny, funny. There are no gates. No, no, no. No gates. No heaven to shut or open. None at all.

Pause.

Eternal closing time.

Silence.

The stupid boy left the gates open that's why the horses were all over the lawn. That's why, woman. That's why.

Pause.

It's not the fences... I know it's not the fences...

Pause.

'Your blessed Mother in Heaven weeps when you do that. She weeps for your sins against her dearly beloved son...'

Pause.

A dearly beloved son.

Pause.

All women are whores.

Silence.

MISS EVANS
>I liked to lay the fire with little sticks. Small dry sticks. I would collect them along the back hedge, not in the wood. Mother said, not to go in the wood. You never knew what would be in a wood, Mother said.
>
>*She shuffles on.*
>
>I was good at laying fires. She said, 'Leave the fire to Bridget.' Mother knew I was good at fires.
>
>*Pause.*
>
>I really liked to lay the fires.
>
>*Pause.*
>
>I'd like to lay a fire again. I liked clearing the ashes, that soft scraping sound when you put the shovel under the ash.
>
>*Pause.*
>
>That is a beautiful sound. One of my favourite sounds.
>
>*She shuffles on.*
>
>*Enter MRS MORGAN, a tall lean woman, spry and active, impatient, bossy and nosey. She carries a handbag. She sits in the seat by the fire*

which she considers her own and controls the TV without any consideration for others.

MRS MORGAN

> Bring me my tea, girl! My two scones!
>
> *MAURA brings her tea and scones which she feels with a bony finger.*
>
> Hard! Stale! Take it away!
>
> *MAURA takes it away.*
>
> Disgraceful!
>
> *TESSIE replaces the rejected scone and MRS MORGAN tests it.*
>
> Better! But not much.
>
> *MAURA goes out for fresh tea. FRANCIS comes in and parks his wheelchair opposite EVA at the chess table as MAURA returns.*

EVA

> Francis.
>
> *Pause. Spot only on them. Quietly.*
>
> Tell me what happened.
>
> *Very quietly.*
>
> Please?

FRANCIS

> *With exhaustion and depression.*

> There is nothing to tell you. Nothing at all.

EVA

> My God.

> *FRANCIS begins to arrange the chess pieces.*

> Really nothing? No reply, no answer, nothing?

FRANCIS

> No. None.

EVA

> But, your cousin. What about your cousin? Did your solicitor contact your cousin?

FRANCIS

> Can't be traced.

EVA

> But the cousin who met your eldest boy, Robin, a year ago remember? How about that cousin?

FRANCIS

> Moved. Can't be found.

EVA

> But...

FRANCIS

> Nothing. Stupid of me to hope.

EVA

> There must be other ways of contacting them.

FRANCIS

> The American continent is vast. If you lose contact where do you start?

EVA

> Did he try the Embassy?

FRANCIS

> Yes. Yes.

EVA

> What about the police?

FRANCIS

> That too. Even that. I could see I exasperated the poor man. He has really tried. He's tried everything.

EVA

> There must be some way...

FRANCIS

> There's nothing left to be done. There he was, trying not to say: 'I told you so.' He's a decent

man, my solicitor. He pointed out that he had
warned me, advised me to not make everything
over to them. To keep the house at least. That
there could be problems. I just didn't want
my boys to be tied like I had been. Stupid.
Downright stupid. I can't blame my solicitor, he
did everything to dissuade me. I'm just a bloody
stupid fool.

EVA

I like fools.

FRANCIS

That proves you're an even bigger one.

EVA

Thanks!

FRANCIS

I just never dreamed I'd live this long. All those
medics shook their dandruff over me years ago.
'You might make it to forty in a warm climate,'
they said. 'Move to a warm climate,' they said.
But how could I? Couldn't. No work for me
there. And Jean, Jean couldn't stand the heat.
It would have killed her. She was extremely
sensitive to heat.

EVA

>I forget what you were like at forty.

FRANCIS

>None of my family lived long.

EVA

>How could I remember what you were like at forty? I hadn't met you at forty.

FRANCIS

>They all snuffed it early.

EVA

>You were smashing at sixty.

FRANCIS

>Mind you, most of them drank themselves under the sod. The best way to go.

EVA

>So that means... you won't be able... that, you've nothing?

FRANCIS

>Was it Oscar Wilde who said, making mistakes enabled you to notice when you made the same mistakes again?

EVA

> *Looking away from FRANCIS.*

> So you won't be staying on here?

FRANCIS

> *Quietly.*

> No. I won't be staying on here.

EVE

> Will you have to leave soon?

FRANCIS

> Yes.

EVA

> A matter of weeks?

FRANCIS

> About that. In about a week.

EVA

> Oh.

FRANCIS

> I'm sorry Eva, what a mess.

> *Pause.*

> But we are prepared aren't we?

EVA

>Yes.

>*Silence. She arranges some chess pieces.*

>We are ready. Some people never arrange to be ready.

FRANCIS

>On then. On with our game.

>*He is looking at EVA.*

EVA

>*Looking at FRANCIS.*

>On with our game. Let our game begin.

>*They start to play chess.*

>*Enter MARGIE, PAUL and MATRON back left, MATRON stands between MARGIE and PAUL. PAUL carries a paper bag.*

MARGIE

>We are glad to have caught you...

>*MATRON looks at MARGIE.*

PAUL

>We wanted a word...

>*MATRON looks at PAUL.*

MATRON

> How can I help you?
>
> *MATRON looks out front.*

MARGIE

> We need to discuss...
>
> *MATRON looks at MARGIE.*

PAUL

> Our concern for Mrs Murphy...
>
> *MATRON looks at PAUL.*

MARGIE

> My mother is difficult...
>
> *MATRON looks at MARGIE.*

PAUL

> My mother-in-law is individual.
>
> *Matron looks at PAUL.*

MARGIE

> Considering her age...
>
> *MATRON looks at MARGIE.*

MATRON

> Mrs Murphy is no trouble, enjoys life most days...

MATRON looks out front.

MARGIE

>You know our change of plans...

MATRON looks at MARGIE etc.

PAUL

>Now we've moved nearer...

MARGIE

>She needs us, her family...

PAUL

>We can do more for her...

MARGIE

>I understand her little ways...

MATRON

>She's quite independent...

MARGIE

>But she's weakening, weakening and the doctor says...

PAUL

>Now she's confined to her chair...

MATRON

>She's contented here.

MARGIE

>Of course, Mrs Price, you look after her so well. We have always had complete confidence in you, complete. But we have to consider many things Paul and I. It has not been easy making the journeys here. That's why, when Paul's job allowed it, we moved nearer, and now she isn't mobile, can't drive any more, we find that the expenses are mounting. We feel, we know, she'd be better close to us.

PAUL

>Things are not easy. No, not at all easy.

MARGIE

>Quite frankly, Matron, the expense... Well things don't get cheaper, do they?
>
>*Pause.*
>
>But the main thing is mother's comfort. What's best for her is the main thing. I feel sure she'll really be happier closer to me. I am her nearest and dearest. I'm her only child, you know.

MATRON

>Naturally, like yourself, I wish only the best for Mrs Murphy. But she is contented here, has good

friends. They can mean a lot when one is getting on. I hope you have carefully considered how great a responsibility you are taking on. I have a fully trained staff. I ensure all my patients are under constant but unobtrusive observation. On your own this could become a heavy burden, day and night, every day of the week. But I know too, that she is devoted to you, speaks of you and your husband very often. She would hate to cause you any trouble. But moving the elderly is most distressing for them, must be considered carefully.

MARGIE

Dear Mrs Price, you've understood so well. Mother is an easily influenced person. She can behave very unpredictably you know. She gave Paul and me some headaches in the past. Oh dear, got up to some mad schemes, putting her little bit of money into some theatre group. Managed to put a stop to that by moving her here. Thank God we discovered you, and this lovely home of yours. Took her away from temptation. Sometimes I think I'm the mother and she's the child.

PAUL

> Margie means she feels she has to protect Mother from herself...

MATRON

> I don't honestly see that she's in any great danger here. We are very experienced with the elderly and Mrs Murphy enjoys company, it's very good for her. Knowing her as I do, she'll agree to your plans even if they are not what she wants. I only hope they are what she wants. I would be grateful however, if you would be good enough to let me know if and when she is going. I have people on my waiting list to be considered.

MARGIE

> We have to face facts. It is going to be impossible for her to stay.

PAUL

> It's sad. But my wife is right.

MARGIE

> Dr Collins agrees. He sees my point of view.

PAUL

> He's a very good man. My mother-in-law has great confidence in him.

MARGIE

> So you understand, Matron, we will be moving her soon. There are influences here you may not be aware of. I have all the plans made. I'll speak to you again, after my little chat with Mother.

MATRON

> You will do as you think best, of course. But I do suggest that you don't rush things. The elderly have their own little ways. But I must say I have never noticed your mother unduly influenced by anyone. She's quite a character. Enjoys life. She won't make difficulties for you. I'm certain of that.

PAUL

> Thank you, Matron. You are very helpful. My wife is a great organiser. Full of plans. She's very understanding. A woman who understands.

MRS MORGAN

> Matron! My bowels.

MATRON

> I have already spoken to Night Nurse. She has your laxative, she will see to you this evening at bedtime.

Light fades. Exit MATRON. MARGIE and PAUL cross to EVA and FRANCIS as light comes up on the chess table.

MARGIE

    Mother!

EVA

    Warmly.

    Darling.

MARGIE

    MARGIE gives her mother her cheek each side of her face. Turns to FRANCIS with no great show of friendship.

    Good afternoon, Mr Butler.

FRANCIS

    Good afternoon, Marjorie. Paul, good to see you. How are you?

    They shake hands.

PAUL

    I'm grand, grand.

MARGIE

    Well, Mother, let's have a look at you.

    FRANCIS is engrossed in the chess pieces.

Oh dear, I think we look a bit peaky. Don't you think Mother looks a bit peaky Paul? Just a tiny bit tired?

EVA's eyes drift back to the chess in order not to show her annoyance.

PAUL

Well er... I don't think...

MARGIE

Interrupting.

Oh yes, she does, she looks peaky. We'll have to do something about that shan't we, Paul? All last winter I worried. Only Paul knows how I worried. You over here, so far away from us. Your family.

EVA

I'd hate to worry you dear...

MARGIE

And now here we are again, winter nearly upon us. We must do something, Paul. We can't leave Mother alone and unhappy so far away from her nearest and dearest...

PAUL

But it's different now, Margie, now that we've

moved, we're nearer. She's very concerned for you, Mother...

FRANCIS looks up from the chessboard at EVA.

MARGIE

    We can't leave Mother out here alone, can we Paul?

EVA

    I'm not here alone...

PAUL

    We just would like to be sure you're well... well cared for...

EVA

    Why don't you both sit down dear? Bring those chairs up will you, Paul?

PAUL brings two chairs and they sit facing downstage between FRANCIS and EVA.

    Thank you, Paul. That's lovely. It's lovely to see you both. And how good of you to come in this terrible weather. You really shouldn't have bothered. I told you on the phone, I'm as right as rain.

FRANCIS winces and looks to the heavens.

PAUL

> *To FRANCIS.*

> How are you keeping, Mr Butler?

FRANCIS

> Well, for an old dinosaur, I'm not doing too badly.

MARGIE

> No, Mother it's not alright. You can't imagine the time we had coming, the roads…

PAUL

> Oh, they aren't so very bad, just the rain, a little flooding.

MARGIE

> It's too isolated here. Too near the sea. Too wild altogether. You need to live inland at your time of life. Away from the winds, where it's sheltered. You'd be so much better off living with me and Paul.
>
> *Pause.*
>
> Or next door, with the nuns.
>
> *FRANCIS raises eyes to heaven then contemplates chess, listening.*

EVA

> *Softly, but firmly.*
>
> But I like it here. I like the sea and the winds... I like...
>
> *She looks FRANCIS in the eyes.*
>
> I like the company.
>
> *FRANCIS and EVA smile at each other. MARGIE shifts with irritation. PAUL is uneasy.*

PAUL

> You're a great nature lover, we know that, a romantic. But one has to be practical, face facts.
>
> *EVA and FRANCIS resume their chess.*

MARGIE

> *In a low voice to PAUL.*
>
> I don't know how she can bear it here. Look at that old man in the window.
>
> *She indicates MR MULCAHY.*
>
> Never says a word. Gaga if you ask me. He dribbles.
>
> *To EVA.*
>
> No Mother, I know you so well. I know just how

you're feeling. How you're putting a good face on it. How much you miss us, and being so far from the chapel.

FRANCIS nonchalantly lights a cigar. EVA makes a swift move with her queen, takes FRANCIS's bishop.

EVA

That settles the clergy.

She leans back chuckling.

FRANCIS

Good Lord. I missed that!

Amazed.

You've taken my bloody bishop.

MARGIE

Annoyed.

Mother, please be serious.

EVA

EVA is serious.

I'm sorry dear. We chess players get carried away.

She smiles.

Forgive me.

MARGIE

> I do understand you, Mother. You make the best of everything. 'Look on the bright side,' as Daddy used to say. But now we've moved, things can be different, better. Now you have a choice, to live with Paul and me, or next door with the nuns. It's grand to have daily mass on my doorstep. I'd be so close to keep an eye on things for you. You could do just as you please, and it would be far less expensive. Far...

Silence.

EVA

> I do as I please here.
>
> *FRANCIS puts a hand on his knight. EVA is all attention.*

MARGIE

> A family is so different. A real home. Where you belong. Paul's and my home.

EVA

> But the stairs...

MARGIE

> Oh, the stairs would be no bother. Remember the little room at the back? You don't realise how

busy we've been. You don't know what Paul and I've been up to. We thought it all out when we bought the house. Well, we've done it up. Paul's done it all himself. I chose the wallpaper. I chose little violets as I know you love flowers. It looks really pretty. You'll love it. All on the ground floor so you'll manage. It's small, but cosy. Really cosy, now we've done it up.

EVA

You don't mean poky dear?

Quietly.

There's no view.

MARGIE

Not deterred.

But you'll have a lovely view of the rock garden from the sitting room.

Pause.

PAUL

I can take you for drives…

MARGIE

Of course, if you prefer the nuns, I understand. I quite understand. I won't feel hurt.

Pause.

It's a perfect place. Such a good staff. Some of the girls here are not quite... are a bit... rough.

Looking at MAURA and TESSIE with disapproval.

Not Matron's fault of course. Out here in the wilds, what could you expect? Barbarians.

She looks to FRANCIS for approval, but he is absorbed in the chess pieces. She whispers to EVA.

Is he getting deafer? Or going a little, you know?

EVA

Whispering.

Oh yes, he's much deafer. And you're right, his mind wanders a little now and then... says very odd things too.

EVA avoids catching FRANCIS's eye. He gives her a pinch under the table. She jumps. MARGIE is oblivious to this.

MARGIE

See what I mean, Mother? This place is just not suitable. Not the sort of people you're used to mixing with. Very mixed company indeed. I've discussed it with Dr Collins many times and now he agrees with me that as you are now mostly confined to your chair, you need extra care. Family care...

EVA

Interrupting slightly desperately.

But I am cared for, I'm happy here.

MARGIE

Of course, of course you are dear. But you'll be so much happier close to your own family. Near Paul and me. Won't she, Paul?

PAUL

It's your happiness we are considering.

MARGIE

We are thinking of you.

PAUL

Producing a bottle of brandy.

And I brought you something, I think you enjoy a drop of this. Got it from the duty free the other day. Hope you enjoy it. Share it with your friends. It won't do you any harm to have a drop now and again. Warm the cockles, eh Mr Butler?

EVA

Oh, thank you, Paul...

MARGIE

> I think it would be a great help to you Mother, getting to sleep at night. Get Matron to put a little in your hot milk. Brandy is great in milk. With sugar, plenty of sugar. Help you drop off.

EVA

> How very thoughtful of you Paul, very kind indeed. Thank you so much.

MARGIE

> That bottle should last you ages. It's very good in hot milk. Helps you to relax. We all need to relax.

EVA

> I wouldn't dream of ruining a cognac as good as this in hot milk, Margie. But Francis and I will share a glass together after supper. Or shall we have some now, lace our cups of tea?

MARGIE

> Mother!

FRANCIS

> Not a bad idea, might be good for our game.

EVA

>Would be good for our game, but later. We'll enjoy it another time.

MARGIE

>It's important to relax. When you live with us, Mother, you'll learn how to relax.
>
>*Silence. Lights on all cast. MISS EVANS has arrived at the chair near the TV, she sits. She is resigned to the loss of the chair by the fire. MR MULCAHY starts to hum and then sing: 'I Do Like To Be Beside The Seaside.' MISS MORGAN, irritated by MR MULCAHY's singing, hops up, strides over to shake him by the shoulder in a dictatorial manner, speaks loudly and slowly into his ear.*

MISS MORGAN

>Mr Mulcahy, will you please be quiet. This is a drawing room. Have you no consideration for others? We wish to watch television, and we keep it low so as not to disturb others. I ask you to stop. For the sake of everyone.
>
>*Turns.*
>
>Such a vulgar tune.

Returns to her seat.

MR MULCAHY shows no sign of having heard anything but he stops singing. MISS EVANS slowly takes knitting out of her bag and attempts to knit with badly stiffened fingers. MRS MORGAN hops up and down changing the TV programme without any consideration for MISS EVANS who is watching. MISS EVANS makes feeble gestures in an attempt to stop her but she is helpless against MRS MORGAN of whom she is a little afraid. MAURA and TESSIE return with a fresh pot of tea. MATRON enters on another tour of inspection.

MATRON

> Right. That tea's a bit strong girls. Put in more hot water. Ah, good afternoon, Mrs Morgan. All's well?

MRS MORGAN

> *Grunts.*
>
> The Pope is on the telly tonight, I believe. We must all watch His Holiness.
>
> *TESSIE carries the teapot over to MR MULCAHY. Speaks loudly.*

TESSIE

> Would you like a little more tea, Mr Mulcahy? This is lovely and hot. Fresh.
>
> *MR MULCAHY makes no reply but she fills his cup all the same. Returns to trolley. Speaks to MAURA.*
>
> What bloody weather. It's lashing.
>
> *The girls exit.*

MR MULCAHY

> My feet are cold. I can't remember, what was it like to have warm feet?
>
> *He peers over his knees to look at his feet.*
>
> There they are, my feet, away down there. They make me laugh.
>
> *He laughs. Pause.*
>
> You try this. This oldness. Come on tell me. What's the good of it? Where does it get me?
>
> *Pause.*
>
> She won't be able to see me when I'm dead. At least she can't interfere with that.
>
> *Chuckles.*
>
> She would have enjoyed that. That's one place she can't interfere with. She'd have loved to be

there with her busybodies. 'He makes a lovely corpse,' they'd say. Damn idiots. What's lovely about an empty skin, falling jaw, no smile? No love. What's that? Love? She put a stop to that.

Silence.

All women are whores.

MISS EVANS

You have to watch a fire when you first light it. Oh yes, you have to watch it. Mother would say to me, 'You watch the fire Bridget. Watch the fire.' Sometimes I would put the poker in and hold the middle up because it could collapse and fall in the middle and that would spoil it.

Shakes her head in sad disapproval.

But when it went well, the little flames would peep out round the coal.

This makes her happy.

That was nice. That was so nice.

Knits, painfully slowly.

MR MULCAHY

'Fires of hell, remember the fires of hell,' she'd say. 'If you do that you'll burn in the fires of hell...'

MISS EVANS

>   Flick, they would go, flick with their hot tongues...

MR MULCAHY

>   Christ, you're meant to know about love. Never taught me a damn thing.
>
>   *Chuckles.*
>
>   I bet you're tickled pink she loved you. 'Sweet Jesus take me,' she prayed. 'Sweet Jesus take me,' over and over again.
>
>   *Pause.*
>
>   You took your time over it.
>
>   *Pause.*
>
>   Don't think you were all that keen to have her. She was a very ardent lover of yours you know. Oh, to have seen her face when she found out there wasn't any heaven.
>
>   *Silence.*

MISS EVANS

>   Then I'd pop a little piece of coal on the flame. Right on the top.
>
>   *She giggles.*
>
>   Right on the flame tip. Feed the flame, Mother

would say, feed the flame.

MRS MORGAN grunts, heaves herself out of the chair and thrusts forward to the TV and changes the programme.

MRS MORGAN

Time for the news!

MISS EVANS

Oh... er... I liked...

Puts forward a nervous hand in protest. MRS MORGAN takes no notice. Returns to her chair.

MRS MORGAN

We should all take an interest in current affairs, keep ourselves informed, up to date.

MR MULCAHY

Cold. You were sensible in one thing Christ, choosing a warm country.

Pause.

Was it cold on the cross?

Pause.

A naked body dying for our devotion? A body twisting in torture for us to pray to? For children to say their night prayers before? 'Say your prayers,' she said. 'Ask God to keep you pure.'

Sweet dreams darling, sweet dreams. A white naked body smeared with blood.

Pause.

A beautiful young man's naked body.

Pause.

Dead.

Silence.

MISS EVANS

Cheerful. It makes you feel cheerful. Happy. You can always feel happy when you sit by a fire. When I sit by a fire, it's like home. There is so much to watch when you sit by a fire.

MR MULCAHY

Did you want to be God?

Pause.

Did they crucify you? Or did they make it up as a good story? You're the hero. Noble and in glory. Easy.

Pause.

Can you see the good without the bad?

Silence.

To know there is light you need the dark. You need the Devil, Mr Christ.

Chuckles.

Your best friend.

MISS EVANS

So comfy. Warm and comfy to sit by. A warm fire is just like a good friend. Good to sit with. No need to chat. No need at all.

MARGIE

Standing up briskly.

Well, Mother. We must be off. The cats will be famished, they know when it's six o'clock. When you think about what I've said, Mother, you'll see it's all for the best. Only the best is good enough for you, Mother.

Leans forward and kisses EVA. EVA puts her arms around her to embrace her warmly as if to keep her longer.

EVA

I know darling, you're very good. I understand. Be careful going home now, won't you? Take good care.

MARGIE

Goodness, Mother, it's not like you to fuss. You know what a good driver Paul is. Never goes over forty. It's all those terrible speed merchants that cause the accidents. So... we'll see you soon, because I'm getting on with the new plans. Bye, bye, Mother, God bless.

Turns to FRANCIS.

Goodbye, Mr Butler, I'm glad to see you're keeping so well.

FRANCIS

Thank you. Yes, I am. Safe journey.

PAUL

Kissing his mother-in-law.

Goodbye, Mother. Mind yourself.

EVA

Oh I do. I do.

MARGIE and PAUL start to exit.

Margie...

MARGIE

Stops.

Yes Mother?

EVA

I just wondered...

Pause.

Now you have this more convenient house, will you...? I just wondered if you planned...? Oh never mind. Some other time.

Looks down at the chess game.

Off you go, dear, I don't want to make you late.

FRANCIS

You mustn't keep the cats waiting...

EVA

And Margie, remember, I understand, I won't make things difficult for you. I won't.

Margie gives a little smile and wave from the doorway.

MARGIE

Bye bye, see you soon.

EVA waves, blows a kiss. PAUL and MARGIE exit, FRANCIS and EVA concentrate on their chess game. MR MULCAHY starts to hum the tune to 'I Do Like To Be Beside The Seaside.'

EVA

Very quietly.

You know what I was going to ask her?

FRANCIS

> I do.
>
> *Pause.*
>
> They will, I'm certain they will have a family. But later. Some time later.
>
> *MR MULCAHY starts to sing; 'I Do Like to be Beside the Seaside.'*

MRS MORGAN

> Mr Mulcahy, there you go again disturbing the peace. Would you kindly desist? Have some consideration for the rest of us who never interfered with anyone.
>
> *MR MULCAHY stops singing. MRS MORGAN changes the programme on the TV again. Again MISS EVANS is helpless with her protests.*

MISS EVANS

> Er... I would like... I do like... Oh, leave the warthogs! I have never before seen a warthog. Very educational. It's very interesting about wild animals... Mother never ever saw a warthog!

MRS MORGAN

> *Grunts.*
>
> Dirty beasts!

MISS EVANS resigns herself to the new programme. MRS MORGAN drifts to sleep again. Snores occasionally. MR MULCAHY picks up his cup and holds it in his lap.

MR MULCAHY

> Brandy, give me brandy. Here's to the grape.
>
> *Raises the teacup a little.*
>
> The juice of the grape, that is a good friend. Reliable. Never let me down. Never. Gave me the last drop of its golden blood.
>
> *Pause. He tries a sip of tea.*
>
> Cold.
>
> *TESSIE and MAURA come back. TESSIE takes MR MULCAHY's cup. They stand each end of the trolley, EVA has her queen raised. MULCAHY stares angrily at the window. The rain and wind lash the panes. Still. Light fades.*

Act Two

Scene One

A clifftop near The Retreat. In contrast to the void in Act One this set conveys light, space, air, life, growth. Colours: green, blue, yellow, white, the colours of spring. Sound of breakers far below. Larks sing. The edge of the cliff is upstage, stage slopes to downstage.

FRANCIS enters in his wheelchair. He is very tired but excited. He is skillful with the chair. Calls over his shoulder to EVA who is offstage. He is puffed.

FRANCIS

>How are you doing? Can you manage?
>
>*Turns to await EVA's approach.*
>
>The ground is level here, we can rest for a while. Are you alright love?

EVA

>Of course I'm alright. I am doing fine.
>
>*She sounds very puffed.*

FRANCIS

>Take it easy. No need to hurry. Are you sure you

can manage?

EVA

Arriving slowly and with great effort.

I'm sure. Hurry? Don't make me laugh. I haven't any puff left.

FRANCIS

Leaning back in his chair.

You're a great girl. Well done. What a climb. I'm exhausted.

EVA

Rubbish. Speak for yourself. You sound like an old man.

FRANCIS

I am an old man. About two hundred at the moment.

EVA

Oh, how you deceived a young girl like me, I never go out with old men!

FRANCIS

There's always a first time.

EVA

It's the first time we've been up here.

She leans back in her chair. Closes her eyes.

How far have we got? Is it very much further?

FRANCIS

Sits up, looks around.

Not bad. Not bad at all. I think it's only one small steep bit, and we'll be there. Well done us.

Sits back.

It's just great to be out, and the day, perfect. Away from them all down there. Right away.

EVA

Opens her eyes.

My God, it's beautiful. Coming up I couldn't look at anything, except the path in front of my wheels.

Looking around and up.

We've nearly made it. I think we might make it.

Leans back laughing.

Great, great. It's great to be young.

FRANCIS

Worried.

Eva, have you got the bottle?

EVA

> Will you ever stop fussing? Of course I've got the bottle, I'd never forget that.
>
> *Pause.*
>
> Do you need a drop now? Would it help?

FRANCIS

> No, no. We'll wait till we get to the top. As we planned.
>
> *Silence.*

EVA

> *Chuckles tiredly.*
>
> My dear daughter, if she could see me now. Whizzing up mountains with her bottle of brandy...

FRANCIS

> Not exactly whizzing...

EVA

> As if I'd waste cognac in hot milk...

FRANCIS

> It might be quite nice you know...

EVA

> It's really good brandy though. They appreciate

our tastes even if they don't approve...

FRANCIS

I'll try it when I'm old, when I'm about three hundred... in the hot milk, I mean.

EVA

Three hundred is a great age to start something new.

FRANCIS

If Margie could see you now she'd say 'there goes Mother, up to her old tricks again. Thought she'd grown out of them.' Has a puritan streak your daughter, where did you get her from?

EVA

I don't know. I really don't know. Her father wasn't a puritan. Bill was a bit stiff, reserved, shy. But not puritan.

Pause.

Funny, when I think of him I can never clearly see his face. The rest of him I can remember. The way he stood, always leaning back as if he was going to fall over. Unsteady on his feet. But his face drifts away when I try to catch it with my memory.

Pause.

FRANCIS

> Jean's face I can see sharply. Even though it's such a long time since she... But there was nothing shy about Jean, was there? Nothing.
>
> *Silence.*

EVA

> Does my daughter understand me at all? Perhaps I am blind to her? Don't help her enough? I'd love to be able to reach her, but she seems to sail further and further away.
>
> *Pause.*
>
> Do you think if she had a child, she might loosen up, relax? I hoped she'd have a child. But she's obsessed by the neatness of her house, her garden, her Paul. Was that because I was such a sloppy housekeeper? Still there's a funny side, Margie doesn't approve of you. Did you notice Paul trying to stick up for you? Saying how nice it must be to be near, as we were such old friends, and Margie bridling and changing the subject.

FRANCIS

> I noticed. That's why I had a fit of coughing to hide my laughter. Should get out my false beard.

EVA

>Do you think they guess how old and how friendly?

FRANCIS

>I'd really prefer a gorilla suit. Would you fancy me in a gorilla suit?

EVA

>Don't know if you'd look all that different. And Matron would put you out at once. She can't abide animals.

FRANCIS

>Hey that's not nice. Gorillas are gentle, loveable people. Often misunderstood.

EVA

>You in a gorilla suit would not be the same thing at all.

FRANCIS

>I think it would liven up the place no end.
>*Pause.*

EVA

>Oh, I wish I could make things right with Margie, I want her to be happy, not interfere with her life. She seems almost... to hound me, to hound us.

FRANCIS

> Rather like being a child again. 'Now darling, you'd have a lovely time, staying with Auntie Mary and playing with your cousins.' You know how she makes you eat baked beans, puts you to bed at six and your cousins are shits. But you have to go. Can do nothing...
>
> *Pause.*
>
> Perhaps?

EVA

> We should push on.
>
> *With slight restlessness.*

FRANCIS

> Push is the word. Are you feeling up to it?

EVA

> *Ruffled.*
>
> Of course I'm up to it.
>
> *With more assurance.*
>
> I'm always up to it.

FRANCIS

> Yes, you're always up to it.
>
> *Silence.*

EVA

> We've got this far. I wasn't sure that we'd get as far as this.
>
> *Pause.*
>
> Down there seems a long way off...

FRANCIS

> Another world.
>
> *Pause.*
>
> It doesn't exist.
>
> *Silence.*

EVA

> Do we exist?
>
> *Silence.*

FRANCIS

> If we get to the top we will see the view.

EVA

> I do hope we can see the view when we reach the top.

FRANCIS

> We should be able to see as far as the islands.
> From the map I'm sure we should see the islands.
> *Silence.*

EVA

You and your views. We'll see it. Haven't we always, you and I?

Pause.

Remember the mountain? Our first one? You worrying about the rain...

FRANCIS

I wanted you to see it at its best...

EVA

Fretting in case the mists came and swallowed the view.

FRANCIS

That place has always been important to me. Special. So remote. High.

Pause.

The world laid out before one.

Quietly.

We should have been able to live together there.

Silence.

EVA

I saw a Yeats' painting when I was young called 'A Present of Islands.' That was the present you gave me that day, despite the rain. A present of islands.

FRANCIS

Not a bad title for a painting. But you can have Jack Yeats' paintings. No form. Must have form.

EVA

Laughing.

Female form you mean.

FRANCIS

Warming to his subject.

Yes, yes, lots of lovely ladies. Painters have a duty to paint naked ladies. What do they do now? Rubbish, ugh. I hate it.

EVA

Matron doesn't think much of your poster.

FRANCIS

What poster? It's classical. What's she got to complain of? It's my room.

EVA

It's not the Botticelli she minds. It's the other one. She came to me the other day and said the woman who cleans your room objected. She had fussed before about the Botticelli and complained to Mrs Price. But she managed to persuade her that it was 'Art.' But the other one, the girl in socks and a hat and nothing else. She didn't think that was 'Art.'

FRANCIS tries to interrupt but EVA goes on.

Matron said to me. 'My dear Mrs Murphy, you seem, er, to have influence on our Mr Butler. Could you please ask him to put that, er, that picture, inside the door of his wardrobe...'

FRANCIS interrupts.

FRANCIS

Inside my wardrobe!

EVA

Yes, then she said you could look at it when you wanted and not disturb the staff!

FRANCIS

Mock indignant.

Disturb the staff! Damn it. If I stuck up a great randy Bacchus it might disturb the staff. They are all middle-aged women for God's sake. Disturbed. By the bottom of young woman? Bloody hell!

EVA

> Well, I said I had no idea what you had in your room. You were rather an eccentric old fellow. But I'd do my best...

FRANCIS

> *Interrupting.*
>
> You'd do your best? Eccentric, me? Wait till I get you...
>
> *He begins to chase her in his wheelchair. She tries to wheel away but she is tired. She laughs and protests.*

EVA

> Francis, Francis, stop it. You can't, my chair isn't as fast as yours, it's not fair... stop it... you can't...

FRANCIS

> *Not stopping. After a chase, his chair charges into EVAs.*
>
> Ha ha. I'm the wheelchair wizard and I've got you in my power. Now squeal for mercy, lady. Squeal.
>
> *He leans out to grab her.*

EVA

> *Trying to avoid him and distract his attention.*
>
> Francis, Francis, you daft idiot, you'll break the bottle.
>
> *FRANCIS stops, suddenly worried.*

FRANCIS

> Good Lord, the bottle. Is it safe?

EVA

> *Out of danger having distracted his attention.*
>
> You're underestimating me if you think your larking around would let me break a bottle of booze.

FRANCIS

> Cheat. Rotten cheat. I'd have had you across my knee in a flash.

EVA

> *Laughing and rueful.*
>
> You needn't tell me. I know you. My mother warned me not to go out with wheelchairs like you! Rake!

FRANCIS

> Rake? Me? I'm your honest garden fork! Your

reliable spade. Your friendly neighbourhood ever-ready wheelbarrow. Wheel me anywhere. I carry anything. Wheel me away, feel free... 'I'm a simple soul...'

EVA

'Who lightly draws his breath...'

FRANCIS

True, true, always sweetness and light. And I'm steady. Never put a spoke in anywhere...

EVA

Francis...

FRANCIS

Quietly.

Well. Only if asked, invited. By someone nice. Someone nice. Someone special.

They look warmly at each other, then EVA breaks away to continue teasing.

EVA

No, no, no, you're not such a goody goody. Remember the Southerby's party?

FRANCIS

Playing innocent.

What?

EVA

>Oh you know, that cup of coffee? It was such a stiff party. Boring. You just tipped it down Samantha Southerby's back!

FRANCIS

>Did I? I didn't. It was the dress. That dress, it was red crepe de chine to a chauvinist pig. How could I resist? That plunging back line. A weak, impressionable man like me. I succumbed. I yielded. Well... at least it was cold.
>
>*Pause.*
>
>The coffee I mean.

EVA

>*Laughing.*
>
>It livened up a very dead party.
>
>*Pause. More quietly.*
>
>Do you know it's the small things, the silly things that count? Not the big occasions. Not birth. Life.
>
>*Pause.*
>
>Death.

FRANCIS

>Once you've done the first, the rest are inevitable.

EVA

> Boring.
>
> *Pause.*
>
> Even love. Is love a bit boring too?

FRANCIS

> Sacrilege, sacrilege!
>
> *Pause.*

EVA

> I don't think I know what love is. Lived as long as this and I don't know.
>
> *Pause.*
>
> Did my parents know? Will Margie know?

FRANCIS

> Our time is so short...

EVA

> Perhaps knowing has nothing to do with it?

FRANCIS

> Just a small spit of time...

EVA

> I would have liked to have felt close to my daughter. Last time in her home she was worried when I leaned on her new cushions. And I think

she washes the lavatory after me. I'm not at ease with her. I'm not even myself. So little time together, and we waste it.

FRANCIS

Nothing else to do with time but waste it. Best times of my life were wasted. Lazy, hedonistic times. With you, my idiot. And if it's one of your small things getting to the top of this cliff to see the view, perhaps we should...

EVA

It is what I mean. Time is getting on, maybe we should.

FRANCIS

Move... on?

EVA

It is proving quite a big thing to get to the top of this mountain. I know it's only a cliff, but it feels like a mountain.

FRANCIS

There's no need. We don't have to go on... It's only our game. You can always say 'pax.'

EVA

We need to see the view, across the sea to the

islands, to be part of a large landscape. Like the peaceful view from your house, your home.

FRANCIS

Home.

Sighs.

Where is that? Gone. Everything gone. Flies away. All that time we spend on our homes. Painting them. Knocking down, building up. Putting in cupboards. Carefully restoring with respect for the past. For those who went before us. Lived their lives in the place. Left something of themselves there. Deep in the stones. They're gone. Then we're gone. Finished. In comes the next man and cries: 'What bloody fool did this job? Old fashioned crap. Out. Sweep it all away.' And there goes your little life's work. Your cosseted shrubs in the garden swallowed by a dinosaur digger. Muuunch!

Makes a large munching sound and moves his hands and arms as if he were a huge digger.

EVA

You shouldn't hurry in a garden. I discovered that working in your garden, Francis, when I tried to get things done. I have never seen a gardener in a hurry. They always go steady, wheelbarrow pace. That is the pace of the earth. So then I slowed down. Made, forced myself, to go slow. To look at things, not to worry if I hadn't tidied up this, weeded that. The garden told me the pace to go. Slowly, slowly, sliding like a snail in my wheelchair. Wheelbarrow pace. Your home and garden was a good place to be, Fran. So what if it was transient? It was good.

FRANCIS

Yes. It was good. You and I always had fun.

Pause.

But it's pointless imagining your children will like anything of yours. My home, with its history, in the family for generations. Felt I added in a small way to their work. It was really satisfying to see a tree I had planted twenty years ago, established. A mass of shrubs slowly taking form. To play a part in a landscape. It helped me to stand under these great trees. I found my true proportions there. That's why we need mountains, you and I. So we can feel our real size.

EVA

It is restful, to be our real size.

Silence.

FRANCIS

> But the future. Forget it. My two boys somewhere in America. Haven't heard from them for, my God, it must be three years... and the house... I don't dare to think of it.
>
> *With anger.*
>
> Maybe pulled down to make way for one of those estates with houses barely a foot apart? They might have left one or two of the larger trees, don't you think? Perhaps I should be pleased that so many homes can be on my small spot of land. But the land, is the land pleased?

EVA

> *Concerned for his distress, changes the subject.*
> Should we move on...?

FRANCIS

> It's time to move on...

EVA

> We can't keep...

FRANCIS

> Putting it off. We're a little afraid...

EVA

> Afraid we haven't the strength. It is time to make a move. We should move on.

FRANCIS

> *Quietly.*
>
> We keep putting it off because we are afraid.

EVA

> Are you scared Francis? That we won't manage to play our game in the end?

FRANCIS

> Yes. No. I don't know. We do want to do it, don't we? You wouldn't rather turn back now?

EVA

> *Looking at him. Pausing.*
>
> I think we should – go on. It is the best thing to do, go on.

FRANCIS

> Yes. On we go.

EVA

> I do want to be up there when the sun is shining. I must have the sun shining when we are up there.

FRANCIS

>Take heed there, sun. Listen to the lady. Forward. To the breach. What's stopping us? Let us fly. We are invincible.
>
>*Quips in Groucho Marx style.*
>
>If we can make it.
>
>*Adds.*
>
>Of course we can make it
>
>*Quips.*
>
>Think of the reward at the top.
>
>*They move in their wheelchairs slowly towards the summit.*

FRANCIS

>Don't rush it now. Take it slowly. Careful, careful. There's a stone there. Mind.

EVA

>I'm fine. Don't worry. My chariot is in prime condition. Unlike its driver. It could flip around Brand's Hatch.

FRANCIS

>How I wish I had my Sunbeam now.

EVA

>	A fat lot of use it would be to us here.

FRANCIS

>	What a car! Couldn't she go?

EVA

>	You were the worst driver I ever met. The very worst.

FRANCIS

>	Remember going flat out down the back road?

EVA

>	Dangerous. Fast and dangerous. A drive with you would leave me trembling.

FRANCIS

>	It was a beautiful car.

EVA

>	When it went.
>
>	*They struggle to the top of the cliff. They are overjoyed, exhausted, elated, high. They gaze out to sea.*

FRANCIS

>	Eva, Eva! We're here. This is the summit.

EVA

> We're at the top.

FRANCIS

> We've done it ...

EVA

> We've made it...

FRANCIS

> I wasn't sure...

EVA

> I didn't know if...

FRANCIS

> All the old fools down there will never believe it.

EVA

> No one would believe we could do it, but we have, Fran. We have, we have.

FRANCIS

> God Almighty, we have...
>
> *They embrace. EVA laughs but is near tears.*

EVA

> Fran!

FRANCIS

> Eva!

EVA

> The view! We can see the islands.
>
> *Silence. They park their chairs close together to look out to sea.*

FRANCIS

> We needed this.

EVA

> We both need this.

FRANCIS

> A world laid out in front of us.

EVA

> A new world.
>
> *Looking up.*
>
> Now come on sun.
>
> *Silence.*

FRANCIS

> *Very quietly indeed. Very lightly.*
>
> It is as if we were threads in an Indian carpet. Too involved to see the base pattern. But now, here, as we look down on the sea, out towards the islands, up to the clouds we...

EVA

>... are two small incidentals.

FRANCIS

>Dropped stitches.
>
>*They both laugh.*

EVA

>No, two threads who weave from different corners, then meet, and a new pattern grows...

FRANCIS

>Some of it is slightly irregular...

EVA

>But good colours...

FRANCIS

>Rich.
>
>*Silence.*
>
>I feel rested.

EVA

>Complete.
>
>*Silence.*

FRANCIS

>Eva. The bottle. The bottle. We have a lot to celebrate. Come on, Eva. Out with it.

EVA

> Hold on. Hold your horses. I had to store it safely for the journey with someone like you around.
>
> *She rummages in her rugs and brings out the bottle of brandy triumphantly.*

EVA

> Voila!
>
> *At the same moment FRANCIS produces a bottle of red wine and holds it aloft.*

FRANCIS

> Snap.

EVA

> You devil. Wine. Where did you get that? Oh good, good.

FRANCIS

> We've always celebrated with wine.

EVA

> All those times together when we were young things in our fifties. Those times in Italy.

FRANCIS

> In France. Spain. All those chateaux we explored. Remember Rambures? Pierefond?

EVA

> It was so good. Fun.

FRANCIS

> This must be the best celebration of all...

EVA

> Oh, have you got a corkscrew?

FRANCIS

> Never fear, I have. Just one second and I'll have the cork out.
>
> *Pulls the cork.*
>
> There. To us, my love. To us.
>
> *Hands her the bottle with a flourish.*
>
> Madam would like to try?
>
> *EVA takes the first swig. Laughs. Passes back the bottle to FRANCIS. He drinks. They both laugh.*

EVA

> Francis. I want to get out of this chair and sit on the grass. I must have the feel of the grass. Let's sit on the grass and drink wine.

FRANCIS

> Your wish is my command lady. Just wait a moment and I'll give you a hand.

He gets slowly out of his chair, takes the bottle from EVA.

I'll put these down safely first. Now Madam, would you like my arm?

They help each other, laughing.

EVA

    Thank you, thank you.

    They sit, side by side, on the grass looking out to sea. EVA holds the bottle aloft before taking the next swig.

    To us, and our wheelchairs and all who push in them.

    Laughs. Passes bottle to FRANCIS.

    This is lovely.

FRANCIS

    This is… life.

    They lie down together on the grass. Drinking now and then. Enter downstage from the same entrance as EVA and FRANCIS, PATSY running. He is an active and agile youth of nineteen MAURA follows. He calls back to MAURA.

PATSY

>	We're nearly there. Nearly at the top. It's great. Smashing. Come on girl, what's keeping you?

MAURA

>	*Offstage right.*
>
>	Oh, me heel. I think I broke me heel.

PATSY

>	Take yer shoes off. You'd be better off, they're not made for walking.

MAURA

>	*Enters following PATSY holding, in her hand, one high-heeled shoe.*
>
>	I think it's broken. I hope it's not broken.

PATSY

>	Isn't it great? We'll soon be at the top. Come here to me girl.
>
>	*PATSY turns around and looks everywhere. Then throws himself on the ground. Then rolls over and grabs MAURA's legs and pulls her down on top of him.*

MAURA

>	*Squeals and squeaks in protest. She is hot and in*

a bad temper.

Will you leave off, Patsy Dwyer. Give over.

Rolls away from him.

Stop messing.

She pushes him off and examines her shoe.

PATSY

Kindly.

Here, give it to me. Let's have a look.

She hands him the shoe.

MAURA

They're me new shoes. Cost a fortune.

PATSY

It's nothing. Bottom of the heel a little loose. Not made for the country though. Leave 'em off. Take your stockings off too. Get the sun on your legs.

He puts his hand on her leg appreciatively.

MAURA

Pushes his hand off crossly, still absorbed in her shoes.

Ah Jesus, those scratches. They're ruined on me. The stones on the path made scratches. Oh Janey.

PATSY

>They're tiny. Sure no one but yourself would notice.
>
>*He moves closer to her.*
>
>Cheer up, it's lovely to be here with you.
>
>*He turns her to him and kisses her. She resists and then begins to enjoy it. Enjoys it. Then she pushes him off.*

MAURA

>Go away out of that.
>
>*She looks around.*
>
>It's very high up.

PATSY

>Have you never been up here before?

MAURA

>Never.

PATSY

>We must go on to the very top. There is a grand view.

MAURA

>*Unenthusiastic.*
>
>I dunno. I'm tired. Me feet hurt.

PATSY

>It's those silly shoes.

MAURA

>They're not silly. Do you always take girls up here?

PATSY

>*Grinning.*
>
>If they'll come.

MAURA

>*Offended.*
>
>Oh, I see.

PATSY

>No you don't. You don't see at all.
>
>*He jumps up and begins to pick some small pink flowers.*

MAURA

>What are those?

PATSY

>Sea pinks. They're for you.
>
>*He crouches down with a spring and presents them to her.*

MAURA

> *Without enthusiasm.*

> Oh thanks.

> *She doesn't know what to do with them.*

PATSY

> Will we climb on?

MAURA

> Ah no, well... come here.

> *They kiss. His hand wanders to her breast as they lie down together. MAURA lies on a sharp stone.*

> Oh my God, I'm crucified.

> *Pulls up her skirt to look at her thigh.*

> I was lying on a bloody boulder. I'm bruised; and my tights are destroyed.

PATSY

> *Laughing.*

> I told you to take them off.

> *He bends to kiss her bruise.*

> Kiss it better.

> *MAURA pushes him away again.*

> Look, I'll climb on a bit to see where we've got to. Right? Back in a sec.

PATSY springs off before she can protest going part of the route EVA and FRANCIS went. MAURA sits up, arms around her knees. She is still in a pet. She's getting cold.

PATSY, coming down again.

Hey, we're not too far from the top.

MAURA

Interrupting.

I'm perished.

PATSY

You'd never guess what I saw. I think two of them old jobs from your home are up there.

MAURA

They're never! They'd never get up there, any of 'em. They can hardly put one foot in front of the other. I'm frozen with the cold.

PATSY

Here have me jacket.

Takes off his jacket and puts it around her shoulders. Their mouths meet. They cuddle.

You're lovely, Maura. Lovely.

Silence.

MAURA

> *Leaping up.*
>
> Jesus Christ, I'm bit. Something's eating me.
>
> *She shakes her skirt, rubs her legs.*

PATSY

> *Sympathetic.*
>
> Show us...
>
> *Looks at the ground to see what's the cause of the trouble then begins to laugh.*
>
> Oh, it's ants.
>
> *Laughs.*
>
> Oh, they can bite like the devil.
>
> *MAURA hops around trying to brush them off, getting crosser and crosser, while PATSY rolls on the ground roaring with laughter at her antics.*
>
> Oh, you're lovely Maura...
>
> *She is pulling off her tights.*

MAURA

> They're inside my tights. The little bastards.

PATSY

> Oh, you're so funny... Oh the ants...
>
> *MAURA is raging.*

MAURA

> I've had enough of this bloody mountain. I'll be late for work, Patsy Dwyer, and I'm bit to death and all you can do is roar laughing! I'm going.
>
> *She runs off the same path as they entered, carrying her shoe.*
>
> I'm off.
>
> *PATSY can't stop laughing but picks himself up.*

PATSY

> Hey, Maura… wait… wait…
>
> *He picks up the abandoned sea pinks.*
>
> Hey, Maura wait…
>
> *He runs after her. Sound of them running and calling fades away.*
>
> *At the summit, EVA and FRANCIS exchange bottles, so when one is swigging wine the other is slugging brandy. They climb back into their wheelchairs.*

FRANCIS

> Do you think Tessie has wheeled in the tea-trolley by now? Just think, we're missing those bloody scones.
>
> *They exchange bottles.*

They will just think we've gone down the strand.
They won't worry yet.

They swig and exchange bottles.

EVA

Spilling some down her jersey.

Oh dear I'm spilling some. What a waste. Matron would say, 'Really now, Mrs Murphy, messing up our lovely new jumper are we? Tut tut. What would your daughter say if she found you in this state? Dear, dear, you are a naughty girl. You do give us a headache. We'll have to find you a clean one, shan't we?'

Exchanges bottles and swigs.

My God she bores the pants off me.

FRANCIS

Knickers.

Takes a slurp.

EVA

Watch your language, my man.

Exchanges bottles and slurps.

FRANCIS

I prefer the word knickers. Sounds evocative.

Exchange of bottles.

Jollier.

EVA

Sounds like school. Brown wool and scratchy to me.

Sarcastic.

So romantic...

FRANCIS

Women have no soul. No imagination. White legs flying over the hockey pitch. A glimpse of brown knickers by a wistful youth... ah...

EVA

Flatly.

And eager-beaver Miss Thompson, whistle to lips, eyes sparkling.

Mock melodramatic.

'Come on teams. Oh come on teams.' My heart pounds with excitement at the memory.

They are getting pleasantly high.

Give me the bottle, you greedy man.

FRANCIS

Nearly finished.

Regretfully.

Should have brought two. But this is good.

EVA

    Here's to all our times together. On mountains, in trains...

FRANCIS

    In pubs...

EVA

    In kitchens. In the rain...

FRANCIS

    In cars...

EVA

    Dancing.

FRANCIS

    Eating.

EVA

    Drinking.

FRANCIS

    In bed.

EVA

    Everywhere.

Looks up. Pause.

The sun is coming out. I knew it would. Now we will see the whole view. Just look, Fran. It's as clear as clear.

Silence. They are absorbed by the view. Larks sing.

FRANCIS

> Time is getting on.
>
> *Drinks. Silence.*

EVA

> It is always doing that.
>
> *Silence.*

FRANCIS

> You would have thought it would have found other ways to go by now.
>
> *Drinks.*

EVA

> Backways or sideways?
>
> *Pause.*

FRANCIS

> Which would you choose?

Drinks.

EVA

Sideways.

Drinks.

FRANCIS

So would I. Here's to sideways.

Drinks. Pause.

I wonder what we would find there?

EVA

Well, I'd find you there for starters.

FRANCIS

Oh, so you would. And I'd find you there too, so...

Pause.

that's alright.

Quietly. Drinks.

You look pale Eva, are you alright?

EVA

Yes. I am. But it's you that looks pale. I expect it's all this drink.

FRANCIS

Maybe it's time to go on... finish our game.

EVA

> I want to leave while the sun is still shining...

FRANCIS

> We'd better get on...
>
> *Pause.*

EVA

> You're right, we'd better...
>
> *Pause.*
>
> Fran, you cheat. You've nearly drunk all the brandy.
>
> *She takes a large mouthful of brandy.*

FRANCIS

> Well, you know me.
>
> *Drinks.*
>
> Very unreliable. A slippery customer. Mrs Morgan is always whispering 'whisser-whisser-whisser,' to Miss Evans and I know what she's saying. 'Watch that Mr Butler, he's very unreliable. He'll sit on your evening paper. He'll snore during the news...'

EVA

> I'm a bit dizzy, I don't feel quite so...

FRANCIS

    Do you want to call it off? It's only our game, you know. There's always tomorrow.

EVA

    There isn't always tomorrow. No.

    She drinks. Laughs. Passes the bottle to FRANCIS.

    Just enough for your last slurp. For the road.

FRANCIS

    To us and sideways.

EVA

    To sideways and us.

    FRANCIS drinks.

FRANCIS

    Ready?

EVA

    Yes.

FRANCIS

    Ready?

EVA

    Yes.

FRANCIS

How are your brakes?

EVA

Laughs.

Never had any of those.

FRANCIS

And your spare wheel?

EVA

Only spare tyres.

FRANCIS

Fool.

EVA

Fool.

They embrace.

FRANCIS

Onwards. Five, four, three, two, one... Go!

They spin their chairs around towards the sea, wheel swiftly over the cliff edge holding hands and throwing the empty bottles into the air.

EVA & FRANCIS

Together.

Wheee...eeeeee...eeee...eee

Silence. Sound of distant breakers below. Gulls cry. Bright sun. Lark song. Lights fade.

Two possible ways to stage FRANCIS and EVA going over the cliff: lights get brighter and turn on audience to dazzle them or EVA and FRANCIS stand and jump leaving wheelchairs empty, the latter would require a minor change in the text in the next scene.

Scene Two

Later that afternoon. Interior of The Retreat, colours: grey to white. No wheelchairs by the chess table, but the chess pieces are still in place. Trolley as before but MAURA is absent. MISS EVANS is downstage right, looking out the window. She turns towards the room.

MISS EVANS

    Maybe today I could get to the fire before her?

TESSIE

    To herself.

    God Almighty, where's Maura gone?

She arranges cups on the trolley.

She'll be kill't. The old wagon will ate her.

MISS EVANS

I'd like to try for the fire, not the TV.

She shuffles a few little steps.

I can't stop her with the TV.

Pause.

It would be nice to sit by the fire.

TESSIE

Oops...

She nearly knocks something off the trolley. Enter MATRON downstage right. She passes MISS EVANS with an automatic smile.

MATRON

Good afternoon, Miss Evans.

MISS EVANS trembles on her walker. Does this when anyone passes.

Mr Mulcahy, I see we're well.

MATRON's path exactly follows that of Act One. The actions are the same.

All correct here, Tessie?

TESSIE

>   Yes, Missus.

MATRON

>   Where is Maura?

TESSIE

>   She is gone to get a clean apron, Missus.
>
>   *MATRON shows displeasure at her use of 'Missus.'*
>
>   She'll be here in a minute.

MATRON

>   I've told you before Tessie, many times. Do not use the term 'Missus' on its own. Never do that. I'm Mrs Price or Matron. I have a correct title: Matron. Kindly address me as Matron.

TESSIE

>   Sorry Matron, Matron.
>
>   *Exit MATRON. TESSIE raises her eyes to heaven. Mimics.*
>
>   'Matron, Matron.'

MISS EVANS

>   It would be nice to sit by the fire.

Pause.

I always liked a fire.

TESSIE

To herself.

I'll bring in the tea.

Exit TESSIE.

MISS EVANS

I always liked a fire. A real fire. I liked laying it.

Pause, shuffle.

Roll the paper up, not too tight. No, no, not too tight. It must hold the air, make nice spongy balls. Not tight at all. Roll the paper up.

Chuckle.

I'd read bits and feel sorry I'd missed them, and it did seem a pity to burn that nice girl's face...

TESSIE re-enters carrying a large pot of tea, slips past MISS EVANS who shuffles on with even more determination although this makes no difference to her progress.

As I'm a bit early, perhaps today I could get to the fire before her. It's better to try for the fire, not the TV.

TESSIE is pouring tea.

MR MULCAHY

> She didn't know everything.
>
> *Pause.*
>
> There were some things she didn't know. She couldn't poke her nose in everywhere.
>
> *Fidgets with his rug.*

TESSIE

> *To herself.*
>
> Where the fuck are you, Maura? Leaving me with this lot. Would you ever hurry up?

MISS EVANS

> I would arrange the sticks very carefully. The little ones first, they catch well. Criss-cross I would go. With two big bits of coal to hold them up at the side and the paper all rolled into fat balls in the middle. Mother used to say: 'Hurry up Bridget, we'll die of the cold.' Mother used to say, 'hurry up.'
>
> *MISS EVANS shuffles. MRS MORGAN enters.*

MRS MORGAN

> Who turned the television off? I wonder!
>
> *MRS MORGAN peers around and turns on the*

TV. Sits in the TV chair. She slyly notes MISS EVANS's progress, does not yet threaten her seat by the fire. TESSIE brings her tea.

MR MULCAHY

'Dickie, Dickie,' she'd say. 'Bring me this. Bring me that.' Sometimes I pretended not to hear.

Pause.

Let her moan.

Pause. Chuckles.

She never knew.

Pause.

She never knew what hit her.

Silence.

I did.

MISS EVANS

One step.

Shuffle.

Two steps. Matron says I'm really improving.

'You are improving,' she says...

TESSIE brings a cup of tea to MR MULCAHY.

TESSIE

A nice cup of tea for you, Mr Mulcahy.

He makes no sign. She puts the cup in his hands. TESSIE returns to the trolley. Enter MAURA. She is pale and distraught.

At last. Janey, where have you been?

MAURA

Adjusting her apron and fussing about her appearance. She is trembling.

Oh, lay off will you? I'm alright.

TESSIE

Fed up and snappy.

So yer alright are yer? Of course yer alright. Thanks very much. Bloody help I'm sure.

MAURA runs to the window and gazes out.

What's up with you?

MAURA

I saw something.

TESSIE

You what?

TESSIE follows MAURA to the window.

MAURA

I saw something queer.

MISS EVANS

>If I get down early, maybe I'll get to the fire. A bright fire.
>
>*Pause.*
>
>Sometimes it goes out.
>
>*Shakes her head at this sad possibility.*

TESSIE

>*To MAURA.*
>
>Tell us.
>
>*MAURA turns away, returns to the trolley.*

MAURA

>Maybe I didn't see anything.

TESSIE

>Make up yer mind.

MAURA

>I couldn't have seen it...

TESSIE

>Janey. Come on. Tell us.

MAURA

>I seen... a vision.

TESSIE

>Ah, will you fuck off.

MAURA

> Must have been that... or... I'm going daft or something.

TESSIE

> Will you ever tell us, for God's sake?
>
> *MAURA looks at her shoe. She is nearly in tears.*

MAURA

> My effing shoe... banjaxed... It's all scratched. I wish I never went.

TESSIE

> *Trying to hush MAURA up.*
>
> Are you going bananas? Would you ever stop and get on with the tea? You're making a show of us.
>
> *Takes scones to an impatient MRS MORGAN. Returns to trolley. MRS MORGAN is trying to overhear. MAURA, looking at TESSIE.*

MAURA

> Don't you believe me?

TESSIE

> I do not. Did you see the Blessed Virgin standing in a bikini waving her rosary at you? Saying, 'Here's your life belt, shall I throw it to you?'

MAURA

>   Shut up Tess, will you?
>
>   *TESSIE puts an arm around MAURA.*

TESSIE

>   Well, tell us, for God's sake...

MAURA

>   *Quietly.*
>
>   I saw them drop from the sky.
>
>   *Silence.*

TESSIE

>   Out of the sky?

MAURA

>   The two of them. They held hands and they were laughing.

TESSIE

>   Who Maura? Who?

MAURA

>   Like flying, but they were falling...

TESSIE

>   What are you on about?

MAURA

>   The chairs were flying too.

TESSIE

Losing patience, sarcastic.

Did they have wings? Did you have a trumpet?

MAURA

What can I do about my shoe? My brand new shoe.

TESSIE

Cross.

Ah, shut up and do the tea.

They serve tea. MAURA as if mesmerised, looking often towards the window.

MISS EVANS

If I had fir cones it was grand. Fir cones catch well. Such a lovely shape, it seemed a pity to burn them. But they do catch great. Then the small bits of coal all over the top. All over the top.

Pause.

I was pleased when I did it with one match. That pleased me. That was nice.

Pause. Shuffle.

It would be nice to sit by the fire.

Continues shuffling.

MRS MORGAN moves to the chair by the fire with her cup of tea.

MR MULCAHY

>She won't have that satisfaction.
>
>*Pause.*
>
>She will never see me a corpse. I saw to that.
>
>*Pause.*
>
>She can't interfere with that. I've won. Won that little game. I could stare at her lying there... And I could walk away and she couldn't stop me...

Enter MATRON. Crosses to the trolley. She shows signs of agitation which she transfers into her annoyance with MAURA.

MATRON

>Ah, so you're here at last, Maura?

MAURA

>I'm sorry, Matron.

MATRON

>I expect my staff to be punctual. How can I run this establishment efficiently if I can't rely on my staff? You are much too slip-shod. It will not happen again.

Notices MAURA is trembling.

What's up with you girl?

MRS MORGAN is all ears.

Are you unwell?

MAURA

It's nothing... I'm fine...

TESSIE

She's OK, Matron. She's just had a bit of a turn.

MATRON

Pull yourself together, Maura. Perhaps you had better come to my office, girl. You are upsetting the patients. Carry on, Tessie. There is nothing to worry about.

Exit MATRON with MAURA.

MRS MORGAN

Loudly.

Listen to this: A conference of five hundred experts called in Spain to discuss the finding of a million-year-old human skull has been cancelled after the discovery that it is probably a monkey's! Experts! Huh!

MISS EVANS

'Don't play with fire,' Mother would say. 'Don't

play with fire.' There was a big, dirty, coal glove to use, but I preferred to use my fingers. It was easier to pop the coal on with my fingers. 'Feed the flame,' Mother would say. 'Feed the flame.'

Shuffle.

I didn't like the coal glove. Made my hands awkward, so sometimes I'd drop the coal in the wrong place and the sticks would break under the weight. Oh dear, I didn't like that to happen.

Pause. Shuffle.

The coal glove was a present so we had to use it.

Pause.

It was a present from Aunt Lily. She made it herself.

Pause.

Aunt Lily could come and drink tea and say, 'I'm glad to see you're getting such good wear out of the coal glove.'

A white faced MARGIE, followed by a horror-struck PAUL, barges into the room followed by MATRON who is trying to divert them into her office. MAURA follows. Their entrance makes no impression on MISS EVANS or MR MULCAHY. MRS MORGAN, who is engrossed in the racing on the TV, gradually begins to think something is up. Strains to overhear. MAURA joins TESSIE. MARGIE and PAUL stand in front of the chess table. MATRON still trying to hustle them away so no one overhears.

MARGIE

Oh my God, what I've heard...

MATRON

Very flustered.

Oh dear, Mrs... I'm so distressed. I'm... Please could you come somewhere private?

MARGIE

...it can't be true?

MATRON

Please come to my office...

PAUL

Oh, it mustn't be true... What we've just heard.

MATRON

It would be quieter there...

MARGIE

I don't believe such a thing could have happened...

PAUL

>Dear God, how could it...

MARGIE

>Possibly have happened?

PAUL

>It's unbelievable.

MARGIE

>*To Matron.*
>
>It's not true.

MATRON

>Oh, my dear Mrs... I'm afraid... you will have to be strong.

PAUL

>Oh, Margie, it's true.

MATRON

>If you'd let me just take you...

MARGIE

>*Angry.*
>
>She shouldn't have been let!
>
>*MRS MORGAN is staring.*

PAUL

>Not on her own.

MARGIE

> Needed more supervision. She was not responsible.

MRS MORGAN

> Shh! I am trying to watch this programme.

MATRON

> I must insist that you come to my office. I must consider the other guests.

MARGIE

> *Not listening to MATRON.*
>
> Mother was getting quite muddled... anyone could see her mind was wandering...

PAUL

> No. She knew what she was doing.

MARGIE

> I saw the signs, she was getting senile.

MATRON

> Such a thing to happen. Please would you come...

MARGIE

> And that man.
>
> *Glares.*
>
> That man was positively dangerous!

PAUL

> Not that bad...

MARGIE

> He was very bad for mother. Quite upset her. A very bad influence. Affected her mind.

PAUL

> No. No. Not really. He was quite...

MARGIE

> I know my mother. She was easily led.

PAUL

> I never thought that...

MARGIE

> Oh, the things that will be said... She should have been with me. Or with the nuns. She was obstinate. Difficult. Would not be helped. I tried and I tried. Did all that I could. I did everything...

PAUL

> You did everything that you should and more...

MARGIE

> She was not properly supervised... to take such risks...

To MATRON.

How dare you let them up there!

PAUL

She knew about risk.

MATRON

You're distraught... You're distressed... I will help you all I can...

MARGIE weeps. MAURA and TESSIE bring her a chair and a cup of tea. MATRON tries to comfort both. More or less giving up trying to get them out of the room.

MARGIE

Help? How dare you say you'll help! My mother was your responsibility. Oh, how right I was to want to remove her. I'll never forgive myself. You, you...

PAUL

Sit down, Margie. We'll manage. We'll be alright.

MRS MORGAN

I think it's disgraceful, visitors causing such a disturbance at tea time. Tea, should be peaceful.

She keeps her eyes on the TV.

TESSIE

> Have a cup of tea, it'll warm you up. Sugar is good for you when you've had a shock.

MARGIE

> I don't believe it.

MAURA

> I told you it's true.

MATRON

> Please come to my study. It would be much more private.

PAUL

> Margie. Let's go somewhere private...

MATRON

> Mr Daly, please persuade your wife to come. This is unsettling my patients. We all need peace and quiet.

MAURA

> It was the truth I saw. I told you.

MATRON

> *Quietly.*
>
> Who was on duty? Why weren't they missed?

MAURA

>I wish it was a dream. I wish I could wake up into a dream. But there's only what's real.

MATRON

>I am responsible. I could be closed.

TESSIE

>*To MARGIE.*
>
>You'll feel better with tea inside you.

MARGIE

>Oh, not tea. No tea. No more tea. I don't need anything. I need.
>
>*Pause.*
>
>I need my mother.
>
>*Pause.*
>
>I need...

TESSIE

>Your husband is with you...

MARGIE

>My mother...

PAUL

>Margie, I'm with you...

MARGIE

> Where is she? I want to see her. Mother?

PAUL

> We'll manage. We're together, Margie. We'll manage.

MARGIE

> Mother.
>
> *Silence.*
>
> I need.

MISS EVANS

> 'Look at your dirty hands,' Mother would say, when I used my fingers and not the coal glove. 'I can't put up with dirty hands.' Aunt Lily gave Mother a present of plants. She would check with her finger to feel if Mother had watered them. Mother didn't know she did that. But I saw Aunt Lily do it. I saw her.
>
> *Silence.*

MR MULCAHY

> *Quietly.*
>
> 'There's no sweet Jesus waiting for you,' I told her. I told her that as she was dying. She couldn't speak. But she heard. Her eyes watching me.

'There's no sweet Jesus waiting for you. No one. Nothing. You're just going to rot in your grave. Turn into dung. No eternal fuck with your sweet Jesus.'

MISS EVANS

I would like to get to the fireside today. Oh, that would be so very nice. If I can get there before her.

Pause.

To sit by the fire. I would like a fire to sit by, me. Fires talk. The flames make that fluttering noise, fire talk. I like to listen to fire talk. Sometimes, when Mother was out, I would pull a stick out of the fire and wave it against the fire-back. It looked like ribbons if I waved it quickly. Like a rainbow. Very pretty. I liked that.

MARGIE stands and moves towards the window. PAUL and MATRON on either side are supporting her. MARGIE moves slowly as if drawn to look out to the cliff where the tragedy happened. MAURA follows. They stand in a frightened huddle. MRS MORGAN joins the group looking out and up towards the clifftop. TESSIE enters back and stands upstage holding a picture in her arms across her chest. She stands behind the group that is downstage. MATRON takes a few steps away from the group. She looks to MR MULCAHY. He does not look at her. She looks away and then looks with the others at the clifftop.

MAURA

In a whisper.

They fell from the sky. From the cliff... from the mountain... Over there, out there.

They all look up and out.

TESSIE

Out there. Up there.

As they stand still, looking out, they have a sculptural quality. MISS EVANS has arrived at the seat by the fire. She sits. She is completely content and utterly unaware of the tragedy. A smile of contentment spreads over her face. She looks into the fire.

MISS EVANS

> I like to sit by the fire. 'I always liked a fire.'
>
> *Pause.*
>
> Mother said.
>
> *MR MULCAHY stares blankly out of the window. He sings 'I do like to be beside the seaside,' for the first time without interruption. The rest remain motionless. Light remains on MISS EVANS and MR MULCAHY. The other group becomes silhouetted. Sound of wind and lashing rain on window panes. Lights fade.*

Acknowledgement

I Do Like to be Beside the Seaside was composed by John A Glover Kind, 1907.

www.ingramcontent.com/pod-product-compliance
Lightning Source LLC
Chambersburg PA
CBHW072052290426
44110CB00014B/1652